TIN COYOTE

JANICE D. RUBIN

BLUE LIGHT PRESS ◆ 1ST WORLD PUBLISHING

1ST WORLD
PUBLISHING

SAN FRANCISCO ◆ FAIRFIELD ◆ DELHI

TIN COYOTE

Copyright ©2018 by Janice D. Rubin

1ST WORLD LIBRARY
PO Box 2211
Fairfield, IA 52556
www.1stworldpublishing.com

BLUE LIGHT PRESS
www.bluelightpress.com
Email: bluelightpress@aol.com

BOOK & COVER DESIGN
Melanie Gendron
melaniegendron999@gmail.com

COVER ART
Melanie Gendron

AUTHOR PHOTO
Nicole Taylor

FIRST EDITION

ISBN 978-1-4218-3800-7

Dedicated to my Father
John Rubin

Table of Contents

I.

II.

I.

Chrome Yellow #5

We hike north, up Blue River
around the dry river bend
rocks exposed, still winter.

Parched riverbed cracked wide in white rock, split open
like the black ink of calligraphy
emblazed on a piece of white parchment.

It's getting dark soon, we need to turn back, toward the trailhead.
You pose on the timber bridge, let your hair down
draped across your shoulders.
You look back leave me on the trail.

Your painting of Heceta Head Beach is still on my wall.
The lighthouse captured in a flash, a shutter, an open window.
Small streaks of chrome yellow #5
a texture raised off the canvas.

Remember going to the village of Yachats
to the Celtic music festival.
All expectations high for the waves
to transport us beyond conflict…
to other shores, hikes, rivers and pathways.

It's Hard to Describe

how being gone for two years
altered my understanding
of time, space and desire.

I moved my parent's
furniture into my 900 sq. ft. 1946 bungalow.
Glass doorknobs, curved doorways
fir wood floors, scrollwork and engraving
on the champagne tinted lamps.

They call it a working man's house
built after WWII.

That morning as we moved furniture
under the sharp blue summer sky
the day cascaded and rose in the heavy heat.

All the glassware mother collected
in five decades of domestic living and working
somehow arranged artfully in my cottage.

The screwdriver the young movers left
by the bed.

Everything seems to have changed.
Apartment buildings on the rise in the city
the end of a relationship
a movie theatre closing
a good friend has left town for the
cobbled streets of Belgium.

Maybe I was gone too long.

Telling Us

You took photographs of cabbage plants
on the evergreen coastal path
art study for a painting.
You said you already had the canvas.
I immersed myself in the ocean mist.

We met again late in the afternoon.
The sun was setting
on a beach full of rocks.
Round amber agates, rusty red stones
white shells of clams and crabs left behind
like lights of the city.
Midnight grays silent and alone.

Resting on the edge of the rocky bank
waves turned round rocks over and over, churning
washed them back up on the beach.
We heard the clicking, rattling
of rocks against rocks.
The bones of the sea
told us to begin.

Lake Paulina

Cold pine morning
steam rises off the river.
I recite my morning evocation
wrapped in the arms of immutable truth.
My entire being plunges into the volcanic rock.

You love this side of the mountain
and can't be moved.
Lake through the cabin windows stretches
the length, breadth of our experience.
Love stretches beyond the lake.

Our last dinner at the China Palace
in the small logging town of La Pine.
Fat shrimp over rice
steaming cups of jasmine tea.
We move beyond sensuality
replace it with a deeper bond.

Looking out the window
of the Greyhound bus
returning to the valley
the sun sets in bold pink strokes.

Spain in December

Christmas morning in Sitges, Spain.
Strong Moroccan coffee.
Music like an Arabian ocean
floats through the curtains in our room.

Blue air and art.
Shadows like paintings
fall across the landscape.
Oranges, lemons, shrimp and squid.
Sangria, citrus bobbing in a glass.

Light reflects, refracts
creating space and possibility.
There is still time,
the sun an orange orb.
December light in Spain.

Wenatchee, WA

A sleepless night beside you
scent of apricots on your pillow.
Lean in toward the northern light.
Sunflowers through the open window
tomorrow you are leaving.

Hours together.
A light touch, a half smile.
What to influence, what to change
social justice and mutual friends.
Blue plate special, down the street
eggs, pancakes, hash browns, toast.
Coffee in the morning.

You left this morning in your blue Dodge van.
Wenatchee, a job directing a social service program
serving humanity.
Surrounded by fruit orchards, industry encroaching.
Migrant workers in the fields
across the train tracks.

Green apples, mountains that touch clouds.
Fruit stands by the side of the road.
Spanish in super market aisles.
Rivers locked cold and blue in your eyes.
Your eyes sometimes a softer
cornflower blue.

You were given education, travel.
You wouldn't live life the same way
the second half.
Everything is gone, closeness, intimacy,
something we had just begun
to negotiate.

6

Indigo Sky

Waves rise, dash against cliffs.
Your innocence drifts
on the great expanse of sea.

Indigo breezes through the open window.
A low breath slides from your mouth.
Crickets in the night continue
long after you become silent.

The curve of your white hip
against the cool blue sheets.
A crescent of the moon over the Aegean.

The movement of your ribs,
belly against stillness
in the early hour.

Distinctions

The clerk behind the counter says
the pot I chose for your shamrocks
is far too green.
The indigo vase is better.
The contrast will allow the leaves to stand out.

An array of elegant glass vases
clay pots, fired, thrown
porcelain bowls, crystal, crockery,
café au lait cups
under a cathedral ceiling.

Out the door with the blue vase
of potted shamrocks.
White flowers blooming.
A drive down the crowded boulevard
late Friday afternoon on St. Patrick's Day.

I place the blue vase
with the green shamrocks
in your stark white room.

Cougar Hot Springs

Framed in the steamy mist
we recline, encircled
by the forest sanctuary.
Ferns soft against our skin.

Mascara smudges around your eyes
moisture beads above parted lips.
You look up toward the brilliant
opening in the trees.

Cold river, your destination.
Imprinted on your hips
rocks, pebbles, grains of sand.
Womanly airs have left, pretensions gone.

Immersed in the icy mountain flow
your breath escapes in one low rush.

Railroad Tracks Across Alberta

My father worked on the railroad.
He was eighteen, traveling across Canada.
Tall, blond, they called him Swede or Slim.
He left home on the prairie of Saskatchewan
to seek a life, build his fortune.

Nothing grew on the prairie;
rabbits were plentiful, shot with a .22 rifle.
Years of drought, couldn't raise much.
His brothers and sisters left.
Boys signed up for the war
girls got married.
He was the youngest;
his mother died of a weak heart.
Finally his father gave up the home place.

He took a job on the railroad in Alberta.
The foreman told the crew
the train would be coming
across the prairie any time.
The train wasn't due
but the young laborers worked
lifting, laying track.

Dust and sweat blazed in the clear azure air.
Summer and hard labor felt good.
Building the railroad across Alberta.
Hammering, pounding, the rhythm
of steel against steel.
Dreams of fire and hope.

Point of Departure

Standing in your driveway
you look into the night, transfixed
study the holly tree, the willow in the yard.
Your small plot of earth.

The cherry tree along the fence
planted for your mother
is just now blossoming.

In the night sky, the Pleiades,
the Archer, Artemis
the Huntress, Diana.
Stars negotiate their positions.

The constellations, Ursa Major, Ursa Minor.
The bears, elegant
yet fierce in the black night.

The North Star with silver brilliance
pierces the stratosphere.
True north
reflects sharp edges.
Brightness falls from the sky.

Two Crows Courting

We stand on rain-drenched soil
watch two crows courting.
You point them out while we walk.

Our weekend ritual begins with
a breakfast of eggs, bacon
toast and marmalade.
Huge swallows of strong black coffee
generous amounts of cream.

We walk at a brisk pace.
Pound out answers
to questions raised leisurely
in the Naugahyde booths of the noisy café.
Silverware flashes
raucous laughter, Sunday newspapers
page after relentless page.

We exchange domestic stories
argue commitment, discuss books
analyze lost loves.
Joke about the earthly realm
laugh about the mundane.
We who resist the routine
of the household
have begun our traditional
Sunday routine.

A Ritual of Devotion

Along the December river
I walk the distance daily
remembering your silence.
Past the single Japanese maple
leaves flush with red sap
much too late.
Trunk, branches, stark black
clearly delineated in the distance.

Your silence now like ivory snow, frozen
a crust too cold to penetrate.
Only our words left glacial, rigid
glistening under the steady rays
of the frosted winter sun.

A Beach in France

The bottle of burgundy glints in the sun
in bright promise of insight
as you glint in my mind, in threats and promises.
I look for shelter from the searing
cote d'azure sun and your windy lashing silence.

The wine bottle lies
with pears, a baguette and a wedge
of chevre in the crevice of the rocks
like my love lays sleeping
on the far shore
of immobilized sadness.

Time endures with me
in measures of sea and sun.
Days filled with green rain memories
punctuate my steps
like trees on an Oregon hill.

Bordeaux perception
spills and dries in the balance
of the dance of day.
Crimson stains
the white seashore rocks.

Pleasure now is taken in wounds
red as wine in light of knowledge.

November in Yachats

We walk the beach, rain pelts
our yellow slickers.
Hoods pulled down
lips red, cold with ocean mist.

Drifting apart now
like pieces of weathered wood
we float on the sea.
Salty smooth on the surface
green, glassy blue beneath.
The ocean draws us further out.

We weave through each other's consciousness.
You chase white foam
patterns skirt across the sand.
Chevrons blow over the beach
like dreams racing at a speed
we barely comprehend.

Rocks piled high on the jetty
jut into the ocean.
We move toward salt spray
the lashing wind, riptide blow us back
to a driftwood shelter.

Casting off who we are for a few hours
not worried about the consequences.
Gulls glide, dive on the whipping wind.
Elements reduce everything to a common theme.
Sky turns slate, waves crash.

In the warm booth of a seaside coffee shop
our hands wrapped around hot mugs.
The giant orange crab sign
raps rhythmically against the sun-dried
boards of the building.

Tourists nowhere to be seen
deserted beach in late November.
Clapboard motels advertise vacancy.

One Summer

I saw you, a tall reed
green, full of life and inquiry
exploring the city, learning, questioning.
You came to life in the blue summer rain.
Air warm with the scent of cottonwood
in small town streets.

Summer flowed around us gently
against bronze legs and arms.
We lay on the college green watching
distant figures, people glanced our way.
I heard your heart beat, traced
your features deliberately, stunned by your beauty.
We owned the city, the river before us rushing
into lapis lazuli.

Wise beyond your years, your entire life
rolling like the great expanse of mountains
plateaus, mesas you had already crossed.
Adversity wasn't a stranger you said.

We rested in the empty apartment.
You crossed the bare room
looked from the window to the hallway
contemplating, creating a place for us.

In the twilight hours we fell together.
Shooting stars climbing gloriously
streaking and fading across the silent sky.

End of September

At the reflection pool in the park
Swans, Canadian geese glide
over the mirror pond
along McLaughlin Boulevard.

Cement sidewalks border the pool
equidistant on each side.
Past, present, exist
within the reflection of the water.

A young father, his school age daughter
walk hand-in-hand.
Autumn nips the warm amber air.
The young girl holds a small boat with sails
billowing in the September wind.

Shadows long and tall
sun low in the sky, light refracting.
They kneel at the edge
of the cement pool.
Voices of children
laughter, echo through the park.

The small boat on the water
captures wind in white sails
propelling the tiny ship
across the sun-spangled expanse.

Their day together continues, ripples
into the twilight of memory.

II.

Tin Coyote

Coyote lurks in fields off Hwy 99 North of Irish Bend and Old River.
He works hard to keep crows and gulls from the rows
dependable ally, gazing over rolling hills.

Coyote spins around and around with the wind
worthy protector, daunting adversary, paper tiger.
His presence, lack of blood, bone or soft grey fur
tinged with white.
His eyes green, gold, sparkle, shine with wisdom.
Canine teeth flash, life not given.
Coyote knows his job well.

Coyote doesn't rest but stands a cool sentry.
He guards young plants which will grow into ripe produce;
yellow turnips, kale, and mint to take to market
purple, green, red burgundy grapes to pour into a bottle of pinot noir.

Where's Coyote's family?
In the mountains waiting for his return
from his long day's work.

Flood

(January 2012)

Rain slides from the sky in glassy sheets.
Sheep and cows stand in water, horses drenched.
The only lama in the field, dignified,
noble in the surging pools.
Cumulous clouds cover half the sky.

Benton/ Linn counties, Hwy 99 blocked
at the Alsea and Long Thom rivers.
Lakes, islands created in a single day.
Shifting deltas on the landscape.
Ripples cross rising streams
in fields of lavender and corn.

Animals wait patiently in water.
Hawks and herons fly to higher branches
of oak and fir trees.
Yellow scotch broom and fence posts
begin to disappear.

Another storm front coming in.
Like tourists, families in the town of Corvallis
watch the river rise to flood stage.

Nye Beach

Sundown in the azure sky.
Gray and white streaks, wisps on the horizon.
The brilliant yellow sun
says goodbye, makes an exit.

Waves consistent, white peaks roar, spray.
The Dragon King's daughter
attains Buddhahood as she is.
Her profile outlined
in the driftwood on the beach.

Children scatter, a barking dog, voices
skip across the sand,
echo in the translucent air.
Now what's to come in the interim?
Transformation at the water's edge
as the waves slide, crash
over the rocky precipice.

Shakyamuni expresses in the *Lotus Sutra*, 12th chapter that women can attain Buddhahood, an eight-year-old female dragon, the Dragon King's Daughter has attained Buddhahood quickly by practicing the *Lotus Sutra*.

Along the Siuslaw River

Railroad tracks twist and spiral around
granite mountain slopes
slide under a canopy of Douglas Firs
around rocky ridges
through canyons and culverts.

Pure stream of river water
flows below the trestle
Sweet Creek, Knowles Creek
tributaries, steep hills and gullies
down a mountain road.

Rocks roll through a stand of snags
stripped of their limbs.
Ghostly shadows, broken trees, stand alone
in ponds, sloughs, lowland streams
off the Siuslaw.

Emerging from the long tunnel
through the mountain
sunlight ricochets
at the end of the dark passage.
Trees, different shades of green
cascade down the hill
meet boat ramps and docks on the river.

Along the railroad tracks
a few horses graze
in a meadow full of wildflowers, blue lupine
scarlet bergamot and huckleberry

Old mill closed, house on stilts.
There was a time when cutting trees, knew no limit.
Mills quiet now, wood dryer pyramid shaped
weather beaten, left standing.

Winding around the North-Fork of the Siuslaw
train tracks roll into the small timber town of Mapleton.
Frank's Tavern and The Alpha Bit Café
appear across the road.

Sylvia Beach Hotel

(Newport, Oregon)

Cozy room of my own
reading the Paris Review.
Tonight wind and sea rhythms
blow through the expatriot window.

Sinking into the soft down of Gertrude's bed
dreams of Paris, busy city boulevards
Gertrude, Alice, a Moveable Feast.
Ocean mist, wave upon wave, salty crystalline.

Immersed in renewal.

Royal Canadian Air Force

1.
Lining up for the military parade
at attention on the landing strip.
Private first class,
sheet metal worker on the B52's.

Silver buttons polished
black boots shine
in the sunlight of the clear blue prairie air.
Creases on his field service garrison cap
blue grey uniform, sharp.
Steel wings soar across his breast pocket.

2.
On a night when taps had played
soldiers asleep in their bunks,
he scaled a barbwire fence to visit
a certain woman.
A young lover in Winnipeg.

3.
That hot summer
hitchhiking through British Columbia.
His weekly pay envelope spent at the beer parlor
raising thick glass mugs.
The Salvation Army greeted him
with pancakes and bacon.

4.
Trading stories with Air Force pals.
Maintaining airplanes to win the war.
Serving together day to day
youth and the hope of peace united them.

Shopping

My mother waves her hands through the air
like an air traffic controller
in the downtown department store.
Just try it on.
In the Fall before school began
she insisted I try on a wool winter coat.
I gave in, put it on.

She tugged the hem once,
twice, to straighten the folds.
Snapped the coat into a snug fit.
Jerked me into becoming her responsible
daughter with a long waist
who could wear fashionable clothes.

A Christmas present, a nightgown with frills.
I wanted plaid flannel pajamas like Dad.
Mother had excellent taste
she spent money only on quality clothes,
they lasted well beyond a second career.

Campbell River

Across Vancouver Island on Campbell River
lumberjacks jump from log to log.
Agile bodies, sharp poles
propel rafts of fresh-cut trees
down the river, over white rapids.
Sparkling drops of river water
suspended in the air.
Dancing on Campbell River
polished silver, iron cleats
glisten in the sun.
Chips of wet wood fly.

I was five years old as I watched the world rush by.
Collected stones from the smooth river banks.
Knew some good spots for pretending.

Sitting on the banks
towheaded and tan, days outside.
We gazed from the mouth of Campbell River
to the calm Pacific, lost in our dreams.

Pop bottles lay in the river ditches
turned in at the corner store.
We savored red licorice and penny candy.
Mother's voice echoed across treetops
calling us home.
A couple nickels in our pockets
brown arms, thin legs, smeared with river silt.

The neighbor's yellow lab at our heels.
Behind us the screen door slammed
dinner on the table.
Today lumberjacks danced
on Campbell River.

Rain on Spring Concrete

Cottonwood, a flash of Spring
on the bike path.
Scent of concrete
rain on the blacktop
on the still water path.

A car door slams
one of those four-wheel drive
pickup trucks, jacked up
in this six-pack parking lot.

Lonesome neighborhood.
Quiet men without jobs.
Baseball caps pushed back
aimless, smoking, kicking rocks.

No money to put gas in the car
to drive somewhere.
Today I wait, sit in the Laundromat
cushioned in unemployment anxiety
reading Cosmo and the New Yorker.

Spring has come to this small town.
The stylish wool overcoat
a gift from my mother
bought last winter
hangs in the closet.

Ancient Vision

Four Indian children
sit on worn wooden steps
unwrap frozen popsicles.

They look up as a lone truck passes
in a cloud of dust.
Eyes filled with the lines of burnt hills
of the four directions.
Sweet orange liquid trickles
dries, sticky on brown arms.

Tumbleweeds bounce off
the walls of the government store.
Plywood patched with old soda signs.

Vacation tepees with a view of the plains
peak above the casino.
Rising, sinking, in the waves of noon heat
pushed out of the side of this hill
like a wind chipped rock.
Warm Springs, Oregon.

North Jetty

Someone built this driftwood fort
each piece of wood
gathered from the beach
dragged through silky sand.
A trail left beside footprints.

This small structure has endured
sun rays, wind, waves and rain.
Knots cracked in the weathered wood
bark pealing off frayed ends.
Twisted, sheared from trees on islands
in distant seas.

Logs, branches, boards
teak, balsa, fir and pine.
Woven together at odd angles
leaning in and supported
like a shipwreck on a rocky shore.

Patches and clusters of sharp beach grass
like spears wave in the wind
grow on the windswept dunes
move with light whispers
around the fort.

The space between the boards and logs
create small windows from
which to view the world
far out to sea.

Shrimp Cocktail at the Beach

Seagulls hover
first one calls, then three.
Ten gulls circle above me
diving for a bite of food.

My shrimp cocktail
in the Chinese takeout box
thrown wildly into the sky.

Envisioning Hitchcock's film, *The Birds*
I run toward the waves
panicked, thinking nature
has really run amok.

The gulls can have it.

Sunriver

Scruffy pine and sage give way to tall firs.
Bold strokes of orange
slice the smoky sky
across the mountain.

Sober black outlines
of the forest subdue the fiery sunburst
as the sun sets.

A vision of you walking
through prairie grasses and sage.
Recognition sparks a slow warm glow.
A single lone pine on the hill
the North Star lights up a corner
of the sky.

We meet beside yarrow
the common blue star
and the purple prairie clover.

Writing now heals
the emptiness of parting.

Black ink on white paper.

Wednesday Morning 7am

Bad news too often arrives
with the ringing telephone
all too early in the morning.
The voice of your father trying to
be most gentle and kind,
mother passed away this morning.

Your mind fast forwards
to all the times you have tried to imagine
wonder, is it believable
unbelievable, tried to prepare.

You notice the spider web
in the corner of the kitchen window
overlooked last time you dusted.
No inclination now to take it down
with a swipe of the blue frayed oxford shirt
you use as a dust cloth.

Intricate pattern spun.
Every moment life continues is stunning.
A farmer rushes to put hay in for the winter
while the summer sun beats down unrelenting.
Now, winter is here too soon.

You'll try to survive
until the pale pink buds of Spring
appear on the dogwood.

III.

La Femme de la Marche

Bright as copper henna hair
under the Saturday Market sun, glints.
Lips red naturally.
A steaming cup of coffee in her hands.
She sips, then drinks deeply.
Life awakens, abounds
from the light in her eyes.

Surrounded by plastic saints
images of holy women and men.
Martyrs on her kitchen table.
She creates modern day icons
with plaster, paint and glue.
They whisper prayers
in sanctuaries and gnostic rooms.

A halo surrounds her luminous countenance
she is a part of this collection of plaster saints.
Italian movies, the life she loves
the passion of *la dolce vita*.
Flying too close to the flames
she risks everything.
Ecstasy has become
her spiritual practice.

She lives life as if
there is always enough.
Her religion keeps her suspended
in the moment.
Kiss of Judas, sun touched.
Beauty burns a mark
on her scorched cheek.

Whitman in the Stacks

At the university library there are two guys
they both look like Walt Whitman.
One a happy Walt Whitman
long white beard, ruddy red cheeks
black levis, black shirt.
He carries a black bag
possibly full of manuscripts.
He can usually be found in the magazine section
watching the boys study.

The second Whitman is pale, stoic.
He also wears a long white beard
almost to his waist, rimless glasses
an off white felt fedora, crinkled at the edges
the brim turned up.
He can be found
in the serious literature section.

Either one could debut
as Whitman from different periods.
Pre-civil war and post-civil war.
The happier Whitman, pre-civil war
before he worked as a nurse in a field hospital
comforting mortally wounded Yankee soldiers.

Reflection on Bizinsky's Hotel de Sens, Paris

I begin to lock the door of my 1946 bungalow.
Between the door frame and the door
the painting has captured my attention again.
Bizinsky's Hotel de Sens, Paris.

The woman in the street
could be Simone de Beauvoir walking
taking the afternoon off from writing.

Leaving her small flat on the Boulevard Raspail
she waits at a café for Sartre to arrive
after his tryst with a student.

Drinking black coffee with three cubes of sugar
she is patient about his late arrival.
Inhaling her Gauloise deeply,
exhaling the worries about night and the war
assured they will have a good supper.

Geography

I reflect, retreat over the expanse
of my life on your couch.
Scan my inner cartography
survey my interior landscape.
Sit up vertical, not horizontal
like the New Yorker cartoons.
Look out beyond the window
memories fly past…

High speed sentiments, slow motion histories.
Rough terrain, desires, deserts among
the volcanic ash grown cold.
Lava sharp, cuts through layers
in rock formations, lines purple and green
sediments and sentiments.

Within the rocky terrain
you narrate, the beginning, the end.
Emphasize landmarks that serve
as a compass for navigation.
I try to leave you with a one liner,
a quip that sums up our fifty-minute session.

Your voice rich points
to the next stream to cross, river to forge.
Sometimes we disagree but find gold
in the riverbed of our conflict.
Gold creates a path that herons and salmon
know by instinct leading to a golden pagoda.

Discarded across the expanse of the plains and prairie
scaffolding made of lighter wood falls away in the dust.
Teachings once useful blown into the east
on a cold summer breeze.

The golden pagoda under the white moonlight
becomes a sanctuary, a single branch stark
across the silver moon.

Archeology

An academic in a long white coat sits at his rolltop desk, looks over his half-moon glasses. We walk across the dusty wooden floor boards toward him. The boards moan and give as only something can that lives. Curtains partially drawn, sharp shards of sunlight light up the dusty specks floating like planets in the history-laden air. Floor lamps and desk lamps throw spotlights within the dark afternoon sanctuary.

books on black oak shelves
titles in gold and silver
leave us wondering

He has been here for years, in this room at the back of the oldest building on campus archiving a copy of every single piece of paper printed. He looks down on the rolling greens from his garret. He is an insider to scandal, life, pulse of the University. At his own pace he saves important writings from every department. Six copies of everything. He and his quiet assistant are only seven years behind, almost finished with the alphabet.

dust covers like snow
our fingers leave tracks and paths
reach into the past

Bike Rider

Riding through the city quiet
in the bright light specter
of early Sunday.

The world is close at hand.
The top of the railroad tracks shine
like polished nickels.

An old Pontiac crosses
the alley between buildings
drifts like an ocean liner
slowly out of sight.

Gold light in the morning on
white clapboard houses.
Red-lipped children
run in the street
alongside me.

Spiritual Practice on a Limited Income

My friend Sarah gives money to people
holding signs on street corners.
Sarah often asks me to stop the car.
She rolls down the window
hands the young girl
with the cardboard sign a dollar bill.
The girl is pregnant and homeless.
Sarah gives a handful of change
to the Vietnam vet slumped over
on the curb.

The young man waving a sign
needs thirty-five more cents.
The middle-aged woman
standing next to the sleeping black lab
asks for a cigarette.

Sarah has a picture of the Dali Lama
above the kitchen sink
in her one-bedroom apartment.
I ask her why she gives money away.
It makes me feel good, connected
living the teaching.

Sarah doesn't have much.
She works as a waitress
in a small vegetarian restaurant
frequented by college students
and anarchists.
They rarely leave a tip.

Ferry from Brindisi to Corfu

Grecian mist tempts the mind
of the languid, blue-jean traveler.
Backpack stuffed
with copies of Don Juan and Alan Watts.
A warm wool pullover
bought at a flea market
last month in Glasgow.

We slouch toward Athens
lost in baklava, cheap drachma dreams.
Waiting for the sea of expectation
to transport us
into whispered paradise
valued jobs, just enough to live on.

Olive groves, ouzo, feta cheese.
Goats on mountain paths lead
beyond small white plaster houses
to the turquoise blue Aegean Sea.
The sublime life: to live in Greece.

Late morning bathing in salty blue
running miles into warm waves.
Sunlight through the air
water not above our thighs.

We meet British expatriates, gone native
at cafés in cobblestone streets.
Entrenched in local customs
formality left on another continent.
British manners still intact.

Shipping across the strait
from Brindisi to Corfu on an overloaded ferry.
Patient like the sea, content to tell our stories.
We forget hunger, down glasses of cheap frothy beer
wait, sleep in the port of Brindisi.
Tomorrow the sea will let us pass.

Delivery

It was not that I made a decision
not to call you
nor that you appeared behind
the thick glass double doors of the post office
nor that you walked down
the marble steps to the sidewalk
in front of me
nor that I was mailing a handwritten letter
to my mentor.

It was not that you said,
he will never receive it
nor that I said, *watch*
I'm taking the letter
from my briefcase
it's addressed,
I'm sending it off
nor that you said, *file it.*

It was that hope is fragile
courage is from the heart
faith is fleeting.

I'll sleep deeply until the sun rises
and the red chrysanthemums open
into the pale gold light of morning.

Canadians in San Francisco

A photograph of my parents walking
down a main street sidewalk
in San Francisco, maybe Market Street.
Scandinavian in his best suit and tie
he tall, blond, slim.
She shorter, dark, wearing a long coat
a cloche hat fits snuggly on her head.
Her dark hair peaks out, her lips red with fresh lipstick.

Just married, they were on their honeymoon.
Both look directly at the camera, smiling, pleased.
The sidewalk photographer knew
they were newlyweds, full of hope
they had each found the right person.

The film *Pathfinder* is on a movie marquee
in the background of the photo.
My Dad holds his overcoat over his right arm.
His left hand looks like it's grasping my mother's hand
but her hand is held alongside his hand.
They don't show affection in public
they were Canadians.

Going Downtown

We wait for the bus in Portland on Mondays.
Mom, brunette bob, form fitting sheath dress, beige.
Gold earrings like clip on buttons
white gloves, red lipstick
black high heels.

The street cars and traffic slowly pass.
Lush birch, willows, elms line the streets.
I remember gazing up at the architecture
buildings built in the1920's.

She deposits her check from work.
In her rich mom voice, she tells me
always pay yourself first, save your money.
Mom likes to shop, but mostly browses
purchasing something only occasionally.

The Enlightened Fly

Holding onto the tail
of the horse.
Moving at a speed
so much greater
than each day's
erratic buzzing flight.
Destination: Mt. Fuji.

The previous day
flitting from the
empty rice bowl
to the painted
porcelain teacup
in the meditation garden.

In the Writings of Nichiren Daishonin, "On Establishing the Correct Teaching of the Land", "A blue fly, if it clings to the tail of a thorough-bred horse can travel ten thousand miles."

Career Potential Unleashed

Flying along these winding river roads
every no brings me closer to yes.
Every yes reaffirms my existence.
Outlines in the evening coastal mist.

The dark line of trees
rustling breezes through the mountains
like tentative commitments.
Briefcase shifts on the seat of my car
business cards spread across the dash.

Careening, barreling, barging
saleswoman, Buddhist poet.
Driven, driving, arriving at poetry.
Orange sunsets burn in my chest
for every cause there must be an effect.

A hand through unruly hair
a glance in a plate glass window
lip gloss shimmers.
Hose smooth on the curve
of a working woman's leg
stepping with purpose.
I am the woman I warned myself about.

Rockets on the Bike Path

Hiking the bike path under the April sun
a blast and a whistle above:
boys fire rockets in the Spring air
aspiring rocket scientists
little Hindenburgs.

A rocket lands at my feet
broken in half, still smoking.
It must be illegal I shout.
The boy with the mop of chestnut hair
declares, *they are legal.*

With the start of the Iraq war
in March, now in full play
this is how it must have started in Fallujah.
I see the boy later at the mom & pop grocery store
buying a six-pack of imported craft beer.

Light Emerging Across Darkness

Painting by Carl Morris, History of Religions

Swirling constellations, a star burst
millions of massive stars born at once.
A sudden explosive burst
in which the heavenly bodies are formed
makes the galaxy blaze.

Faint light emerges
opal particles of sun
from the dark universe.
Pulse quickens, sky unfathomable.
Icy flash of determination
surfaces from the great ink-blue canvas.

Become luminous star, shine
on the shaded intentions of small lives.
Appear across darkness, burn golden and silver.
Illuminate the path of hope
never extinguished
across vast sky and land.

Traveling from Taos to Portland

Sitting next to me on the Greyhound bus
a young man with a topknot
left a commune outside of Salinas.
He was called Jade;
his eyes reflect shades of aqua green.
Worked to the bone, worked for free.
Rising before dawn, three am
meditation and prayer.

Swept the ashram corner to corner
made hot bread boules`
thick vegetable stew
for the late afternoon meal.

Tilled the soil, plowed fields, reaped
pumpkins in the Fall.
Christmas trees in Winter
picked spinach in the Spring
harvested corn from the fields in Summer.

To bed by seven pm, an exercise in right mindfulness.
Frost on the windows in the early hours, rising again.
Working into the late afternoon until
the sun turned brilliant red.

The Longest Goodbye

The ship pulls out from the bay.
Fog is closing in now.
Whistles and horns
echo loudly over the cities we leave.

India, Morocco, Tangiers, Barcelona
warm countries, cities, ports.
Dusty streets beckon
the wool wrapped traveler.
We have said goodbye many times.

People we know see us drift
into the great distance of the horizon.
We stand at the ship's railing
until friends and family, become small dark points
against the white painted boards
of the old marina.

Sun cuts through clouds.
The movement on the docks and the logs of the pier
are outlined in the morning pearl of light.

We begin again to think of the expressions
a smile, lines in a familiar face
of those we love, those who have loved us.
A moment which echoes with sheer joy, off the cliffs
down the ship's dark passages
into the light of day.

Hiroshima 50th Anniversary

I

Wind twists, turns paper cranes
pink, red, orange strung together.
Social activists carrying children
scattered under the park shelter.
Gathering of the concerned
those who lived through WWII
along with dread-haired youth
still fighting the old fights.

Native American woman of the
Kalapuya tribe speaks
looks out beyond the crowd
talks about the old ones
in New York and Chicago
dying from the heat.
The little girl with asthma
it hurts when she breathes.

Everything has changed
her people decimated
lines in her face deep
black hair streaked with grey.
Radiation has destroyed
the thyroids of the salmon
swimming in circles
they don't know where to spawn.

Laid out on the picnic tables
tomatoes, zucchini, bell peppers.
Tahini and tabouli in recycled containers.
From the river which flows through the city
transients arrive, children, elderly citizens, homeless men.
Native Americans, Japanese all eat together.

II
Manhattan Project

A physics professor from this small town's college
sits on a park bench, transfixed.
The irony of his life astonishes him
leaves him stunned.
He floats like a particle of dust
between a moment 50 years ago and the present moment.
He worked on the Manhattan project, anonymous
he looks around the gathering.

III
Nagasaki, Hiroshima

The last speaker survived the bombing of Hiroshima
bright morning, blue skies, sunshine.
He heard the sound of airplanes
looked out the window and saw three B29's.
Sleek silver pens, streaked across the blue summer sky
sunshine glinting off wings.
A blast of red and orange like a sunset
then pink and it was dark as midnight.

He felt pressure across his body
hid under his school desk.
Equations written on the blackboard E=MC squared.
His hands covered his eyes, ears sticky with wet blood.
Many small cuts from flying glass
blown inward from the window.
Slow motion, millions of points of light and dust.
Matter cascaded inward, down upon itself imploding
beautiful but deadly.
Yeats predicted, the center cannot hold.
Nothing left of the building
but the first and second floor beams.
His schoolmates dead or dying.

IV
Aftermath

Small Japanese man, western bolo tie
polished amber agate, sky blue jacket
he apologizes before he tells his story.
He doesn't want to offend anyone
not the pentagon, the white house or the military.

He describes the twelve- and thirteen-year-old boys
drafted early that year.
Their duty to clean up the center of the city.
That morning, the skin dripped, peeled off their bodies.
Puffed and swollen, they would soon die.
They walked like ghosts.

He looked towards Hiroshima, the old city
saw black smoke curling into the clouds.
He begins to cry, he suffered with fever, diarrhea for two weeks
his body shed the radiation.
Summer morning, the red and orange explosion
the mushroom cloud
the pink aftermath, the final darkness
all indelibly imprinted in his mind's eye.

Elegy for a Writer
(for Carl)

Your writer's hands hold a moleskin journal
and a fountain pen.
You roll tobacco, scent of Amsterdam.
Travelers roll their first Drum cigarette
along the canals by the Van Gogh museum.

We meet at the public library
or the post office downtown.
A daily ritual, checking for letters
from your pen pals, all over the world.
A friend in Australia
you plan to visit someday.

Dismounting our bicycles
we talk passionately about books
go for Chinese food and to the only bar in town
for glasses of beer.
You lament the lack of love interests
seem distracted.
Too many pretty boys absorbed
in their own beauty.

Gesturing expansively you leave an impression
as you tell colorful stories
later written down and sent off
to obscure literary journals.

I remember the night you made garlic black beans.
You looked up inquisitively
over thick tortoise shell glasses, checking my reaction
to your dramatic declarations.

You showed feelings unabashedly.
What happened in Seattle, three strikes against you
gay, black and flamboyant.
You suffered at least one breakdown.

Handsome, beautiful man
you didn't want anyone to know you were dying.
A visit to see you, snow falling steadily
like a soft white comforter
covering the rolling hills outside your room.

Have you moved to another country, another city?
Amsterdam or Berlin again?
I look back five years, an inscription
in a book you gave me *"City of Night" by John Rechy.*
Happy Birthday, this is a classic introduction
to the gay world of the sixties.
It's a wonderful book, do follow Miss Destiny.

Shotgun Creek

Hiking in early December
trail crunches
frozen under our feet.
Scattered branches, cracked wide open.
Strips of wood bark split, white, rust red
broken trunks skewed across the path.

Creek gurgles near the trail.
Salamander the color of brown earth
lies still, then skitters, flips over.
Orange belly bright, smooth
slight pulse of life, eyes flicker.

Moss and huge foxtail ferns
graze our hands
as we pass by trampling
the frosted ground.
Underfoot Douglas Fir needles and Oak leaves.

Small stream trickles down
from the hills onto the foot path.
We stumble, step into mud
then jump and skip over
flat black stones and craggy rocks.

Remember hiking last summer
in the heat of August; you wore
your Yankees ball cap backward;
blue bottles of water kept us cool.
We talked of plunging into
the icy creek below.

Rainstorms have left trees
bent and broken.
Winter air like ice glazes over us
encasing ferns and trees.

White snow dusts the hills.
Sunlight streams through
lights up treetops above the creek.
We run and slide down the way
as long shadows fall.

About the Author

Janice D. Rubin is a counselor and educator. She received her M.S. from the University of Oregon and her B.A. in English Literature. Her poems have been published in the *Austin International Poetry Festival Anthology, Tiger's Eye Poetry Journal, Glass: A Journal of Poetry, Arabesque Journal, The Quizzical Chair Anthology*, (Uttered Chaos Press) the Anthology *It Demands a Wildness of Me* (Uttered Chaos Press) and other journals. She was nominated for the Pushcart Poetry Prize in 2008. She's taught at Oregon State University and currently teaches at Lane Community College. She's the author of *Transcending Damnation Creek Trail & Other Poems* (Flutter Press 2010). *Tin Coyote* is her second book of poems.

Acknowledgments

Grateful acknowledgment is made to the editors of the following journals and anthologies in which these poems or earlier versions of them appeared.

Austin International Poetry Festival Anthology: "Shrimp Cocktail at the Beach"

Kind of a Hurricane Press Anthology: "Campbell River"

Tiger's Eye Press Broadside: "Bike Rider"

Digging Anthology: "Archeology", "La Femme de la Marche"

Rattle Snake Review: "Distinctions"

New Mirage Quarterly: "Cougar Hot Springs"

New Beginnings Anthology: "One Summer", "Geography"

Arabesques Journal of Poetry: "Hiroshima, 50th Anniversary", "The Enlightened Fly", "Rockets on the Bike Path"

HerStory Anthology: "Career Potential Unleashed"

Completion, Compilation Anthology: "A Beach in France", "Light Emerging From Darkness"

HIMS Anthology: "Traveling from Taos to Portland", "Whitman in the Stacks", "Elegy for a Writer (for Carl)"

Songs of Ourselves Poetry Anthology: "The Longest Goodbye"

Poet, an International Monthly: "A Ritual of Devotion"